LEGENDS BIOGRAPHY

BRATESH KUMAR SINGH

I would thanks to some people for this book @N.P. , Mr. Amit Chauhan Singh Sir , Mr. Brajesh Kumar Sharma Sir , Mr. Mahesh Kumar , Mr. Sarvesh Kumari , Mr. Ramji Lal , Mr. Suresh Kumar Singh, Ms. Pooja Singh , Brajesh Singh

Contents

CHAPTER ONE

Srinivasa Ramanujan

Srinivasa Ramanujan

Srinivasa Ramanujan was one of India's greatest mathematical geniuses. He made substantial contributions to the analytical theory of numbers and worked on elliptic functions, continued fractions, and infinite series.

Ramanujan was born in his grandmother's house in Erode, a small village about 400 km southwest of Madras (now Chennai). When Ramanujan was a year old his mother took him to the town of Kumbakonam, about 160 km nearer Madras. His father worked in Kumbakonam as a clerk in a cloth merchant's shop. In December 1889 he contracted smallpox.

When he was nearly five years old, Ramanujan entered the primary school in Kumbakonam although he would attend several different primary schools before entering the Town High School in Kumbakonam in January 1898. At the Town High School, Ramanujan was to do well in all his school subjects and showed himself an able all round scholar. In 1900 he began to work on his own on mathematics summing geometric and arithmetic series.

Ramanujan was shown how to solve cubic equations in 1902 and he went on to find his own method to solve the quartic. The following year, not knowing that the quintic could not be solved by radicals, he tried (and of course failed) to solve the quintic.

It was in the Town High School that Ramanujan came across a mathematics book by G S Carr called Synopsis of elementary results in pure mathematics. This book, with its very concise style, allowed Ramanujan to teach himself mathematics, but the style of the book was to have a rather unfortunate effect on the way Ramanujan was later to write down mathematics since it provided the only model that he had of written mathematical arguments. The book contained theorems, formulae and short proofs. It also contained an index to papers on pure mathematics which had been published in the European Journals of Learned Societies during the first half of the 19th century. The book, published in 1886, was of course well out of date by the time Ramanujan used it.

By 1904 Ramanujan had begun to undertake deep research. He investigated the series \sum (\large\frac{1}{n}\normalsize)Σ(n1) and calculated Euler's constant to 15 decimal places. He began to study the Bernoulli numbers, although this was entirely his own independent discovery.

Ramanujan, on the strength of his good school work, was given a scholarship to the Government College in Kumbakonam which he entered in 1904. However the following year his scholarship was not renewed because Ramanujan devoted more and more of his time to mathematics and neglected his other subjects. Without money he was soon in difficulties and, without telling his parents, he ran away to the town of Vizagapatnam about 650 km north of Madras. He continued his mathematical work, however, and at this time he worked on hypergeometric series and investigated relations between integrals and series. He was to discover later that he had been studying elliptic functions.

In 1906 Ramanujan went to Madras where he entered Pachaiyappa's College. His aim was to pass the First Arts examination which would allow him to be admitted to the University of Madras. He attended lectures at Pachaiyappa's College but became ill after three months study. He took the First Arts examination after having left the course. He passed in mathematics but failed all his other subjects and therefore failed the examination. This meant that he could not enter the University of Madras. In the following years he worked on mathematics developing his own ideas without any help and without any real idea of the then current research topics other than that provided by Carr's book.

Continuing his mathematical work Ramanujan studied continued fractions and divergent series in 1908. At this stage he became seriously ill again and underwent an operation in April 1909 after which he took him some considerable time to recover. He married on 14 July 1909 when his mother arranged for him to marry a ten year old girl S Janaki Ammal. Ramanujan did not live with his wife, however, until she was twelve years old.

Ramanujan continued to develop his mathematical ideas and began to pose problems and solve problems in the Journal of the Indian Mathematical Society. He devoloped relations between elliptic modular equations in 1910. After publication of a brilliant research paper on Bernoulli numbers in 1911 in the Journal of the Indian Mathematical Society he gained recognition for his work. Despite his lack of a university education, he was becoming well known in the Madras area as a mathematical genius.

In 1911 Ramanujan approached the founder of the Indian Mathematical Society for advice on a job. After this he was appointed to his first job, a temporary post in the Accountant General's Office in Madras. It was then suggested that he approach Ramachandra Rao who was a Collector at Nellore. Ramachandra Rao was a founder member of the Indian Mathematical Society who had helped start the mathematics library. He writes in :-

A short uncouth figure, stout, unshaven, not over clean, with one conspicuous feature-shining eyes- walked in with a frayed notebook under his arm. He was miserably poor. ... He opened his book and began to explain some of his discoveries. I saw quite at once that there was something out of the way; but my knowledge did not permit me to judge whether he talked sense or nonsense. ... I asked him what he wanted. He said he wanted a pittance to live on so that he might pursue his researches.

Ramachandra Rao told him to return to Madras and he tried, unsuccessfully, to arrange a scholarship for Ramanujan. In 1912 Ramanujan applied for the post of clerk in the accounts section of the Madras Port Trust. In his letter of application he wrote :-

I have passed the Matriculation Examination and studied up to the First Arts but was prevented from pursuing my studies further owing to several untoward circumstances. I have, however, been devoting all my time to Mathematics and developing the subject.

Despite the fact that he had no university education, Ramanujan was clearly well known to the university mathematicians in Madras for, with his letter of application, Ramanujan included a reference from E W Middlemast who was the Professor of Mathematics at The Presidency College in Madras. Middlemast, a graduate of St John's College, Cambridge, wrote :-

I can strongly recommend the applicant. He is a young man of quite exceptional capacity in mathematics and especially in work relating to numbers. He has a natural aptitude for computation and is very quick at figure work.

On the strength of the recommendation Ramanujan was appointed to the post of clerk and began his duties on 1 March 1912. Ramanujan was quite lucky to have a number of people working round him with a training in mathematics. In fact the Chief Accountant for the Madras Port Trust, S N Aiyar, was trained as a mathematician and published a paper On the distribution of primes in 1913 on Ramanujan's work. The professor of civil engineering at the Madras Engineering College C L T Griffith was also interested in Ramanujan's abilities and, having been educated at University College London, knew the professor of mathematics there, namely M J M Hill. He wrote to Hill on 12 November 1912 sending some of Ramanujan's work and a copy of his 1911 paper on Bernoulli numbers.

Hill replied in a fairly encouraging way but showed that he had failed to understand Ramanujan's results on divergent series. The recommendation to Ramanujan that he read Bromwich's Theory of infinite series did not please Ramanujan much. Ramanujan wrote to E W Hobson and H F Baker trying to interest them in his results but neither replied. In January 1913

Ramanujan wrote to G H Hardy having seen a copy of his 1910 book Orders of infinity. In Ramanujan's letter to Hardy he introduced himself and his work [10]:-

I have had no university education but I have undergone the ordinary school course. After leaving school I have been employing the spare time at my disposal to work at mathematics. I have not trodden through the conventional regular course which is followed in a university course, but I am striking out a new path for myself. I have made a special investigation of divergent series in general and the results I get are termed by the local mathematicians as 'startling'.

Hardy, together with Littlewood, studied the long list of unproved theorems which Ramanujan enclosed with his letter. On 8 February he replied to Ramanujan , the letter beginning:-

I was exceedingly interested by your letter and by the theorems which you state. You will however understand that, before I can judge properly of the value of what you have done, it is essential that I should see proofs of some of your assertions. Your results seem to me to fall into roughly three classes:

(1) there are a number of results that are already known, or easily deducible from known theorems;

(2) there are results which, so far as I know, are new and interesting, but interesting rather from their curiosity and apparent difficulty than their importance;

(3) there are results which appear to be new and important...

Ramanujan was delighted with Hardy's reply and when he wrote again he said :-

I have found a friend in you who views my labours sympathetically. ... I am already a half starving man. To preserve my brains I want food and this is my first consideration. Any sympathetic letter from you will be helpful to me here to get a scholarship either from the university of from the government.

Indeed the University of Madras did give Ramanujan a scholarship in May 1913 for two years and, in 1914, Hardy brought Ramanujan to Trinity College, Cambridge, to begin an extraordinary collaboration. Setting this up was not an easy matter. Ramanujan was an orthodox Brahmin and so was a strict vegetarian. His religion should have prevented him from travelling but this difficulty was overcome, partly by the work of E H Neville who was a colleague of Hardy's at Trinity College and who met with Ramanujan while lecturing in India.

Ramanujan sailed from India on 17 March 1914. It was a calm voyage except for three days on which Ramanujan was seasick. He arrived in London on 14 April 1914 and was met by Neville. After four days in London they went to Cambridge and Ramanujan spent a couple of weeks in Neville's home before moving into rooms in Trinity College on 30th April. Right from the beginning, however, he had problems with his diet. The outbreak of World War I made obtaining special items of food harder and it was not long before Ramanujan had health problems.

Right from the start Ramanujan's collaboration with Hardy led to important results. Hardy was, however, unsure how to approach the problem of Ramanujan's lack of formal education. He wrote :-

What was to be done in the way of teaching him modern mathematics? The limitations of his knowledge were as startling as its profundity.

Littlewood was asked to help teach Ramanujan rigorous mathematical methods. However he said :-

... that it was extremely difficult because every time some matter, which it was thought that Ramanujan needed to know, was mentioned, Ramanujan's response was an avalanche of original ideas which made it almost impossible for Littlewood to persist in his original intention.

The war soon took Littlewood away on war duty but Hardy remained in Cambridge to work with Ramanujan. Even in his first winter in England, Ramanujan was ill and he wrote in March 1915 that he had been ill due to the winter weather and had not been able to publish anything for five months. What he did publish was the work he did in England, the decision having been made that the results he had obtained while in India, many of which he had communicated to Hardy in his letters, would not be published until the war had ended.

On 16 March 1916 Ramanujan graduated from Cambridge with a Bachelor of Arts by Research (the degree was called a Ph.D. from 1920). He had been allowed to enrol in June 1914 despite not having the proper qualifications. Ramanujan's dissertation was on Highly composite numbers and consisted of seven of his papers published in England.

Ramanujan fell seriously ill in 1917 and his doctors feared that he would die.

He did improve a little by September but spent most of his time in various nursing homes. In February 1918 Hardy wrote :-

Batty Shaw found out, what other doctors did not know, that he had undergone an operation about four years ago. His worst theory was that this had really been for the removal of a malignant growth, wrongly diagnosed. In view of the fact that Ramanujan is no worse than six months ago, he has now abandoned this theory - the other doctors never gave it any support. Tubercle has been the provisionally accepted theory, apart from this, since the original idea of gastric ulcer was given up. ... Like all Indians he is fatalistic, and it is terribly hard to get him to take care of himself.

On 18 February 1918 Ramanujan was elected a fellow of the Cambridge Philosophical Society and then three days later, the greatest honour that he would receive, his name appeared on the list for election as a fellow of the Royal Society of London. He had been proposed by an impressive list of mathematicians, namely Hardy, MacMahon, Grace, Larmor, Bromwich, Hobson, Baker, Littlewood, Nicholson, Young, Whittaker, Forsyth and Whitehead. His election as a fellow of the Royal Society was confirmed on 2 May 1918, then on 10 October 1918 he was elected a Fellow of Trinity College Cambridge, the fellowship to run for six years.

The honours which were bestowed on Ramanujan seemed to help his health improve a little and he renewed his effors at producing mathematics. By the end of November 1918 Ramanujan's health had greatly improved. Hardy wrote in a letter :-

I think we may now hope that he has turned to corner, and is on the road to a real recovery. His temperature has ceased to be irregular, and he has gained nearly a stone in weight. ... There has never been any sign of any diminuation in his extraordinary mathematical talents. He has produced less, naturally, during his illness but the quality has been the same. ....

He will return to India with a scientific standing and reputation such as no Indian has enjoyed before, and I am confident that India will regard him as the treasure he is. His natural simplicity and modesty has never been affected in the least by success - indeed all that is wanted is to get him to realise that he really is a success.

Ramanujan sailed to India on 27 February 1919 arriving on 13 March. However his health was very poor and, despite medical treatment, he died there the following year.

The letters Ramanujan wrote to Hardy in 1913 had contained many fascinating results. Ramanujan worked out the Riemann series, the elliptic integrals, hypergeometric series and functional equations of the zeta function. On the other hand he had only a vague idea of what constitutes a mathematical proof. Despite many brilliant results, some of his theorems on prime numbers were completely wrong.

Ramanujan independently discovered results of Gauss, Kummer and others on hypergeometric series. Ramanujan's own work on partial sums and products of hypergeometric series have led to major development in the topic. Perhaps his most famous work was on the number $p(n)$ of partitions of an integer nn into summands. MacMahon had produced tables of the value of $p(n)p(n)$ for small numbers nn, and Ramanujan used this numerical data to conjecture some remarkable properties some of which he proved using elliptic functions. Other were only proved after Ramanujan's death.

In a joint paper with Hardy, Ramanujan gave an asymptotic formula for $p(n)p(n)$. It had the remarkable property that it appeared to give the correct value of $p(n)p(n)$, and this was later proved by Rademacher.

Ramanujan left a number of unpublished notebooks filled with theorems that mathematicians have continued to study. G N Watson, Mason Professor of Pure Mathematics at Birmingham from 1918 to 1951 published 14 papers under the general title Theorems stated by Ramanujan and in all he published nearly 30 papers which were inspired by Ramanujan's work. Hardy passed on to Watson the large number of manuscripts of Ramanujan that he had, both written before 1914 and some written in Ramanujan's last year in India before his death.

CHAPTER TWO

Albert Einstein

Albert Einstein

Albert Einstein was born at Ulm, in Württemberg, Germany, on March 14, 1879. Six weeks later the family moved to Munich, where he later on began his schooling at the Luitpold Gymnasium. Later, they moved to Italy and Albert continued his education at Aarau, Switzerland and in 1896 he entered the Swiss Federal Polytechnic School in Zurich to be trained as a teacher in physics and mathematics. In 1901, the year he gained his diploma, he acquired Swiss citizenship tand, as he was unable to find a teaching post, he accepted a position as technical assistant in the Swiss

Patent Office. In 1905 he obtained his doctor's degree.

During his stay at the Patent Office, and in his spare time, he produced much of his remarkable work and in 1908 he was appointed Privatdozent in Berne. In 1909 he became Professor Extraordinary at Zurich, in 1911 Professor of Theoretical Physics at Prague, returning to Zurich in the following year to fill a similar post. In 1914 he was appointed Director of the Kaiser Wilhelm Physical Institute and Professor in the University of Berlin. He became a German citizen in 1914 and remained in Berlin until 1933 when he renounced his citizenship for political reasons and emigrated to America to take the position of Professor of Theoretical Physics at Princeton*. He became a United States citizen in 1940 and retired from his post in 1945.

After World War II, Einstein was a leading figure in the World Government Movement, he was offered the Presidency of the State of Israel, which he declined, and he collaborated with Dr. Chaim Weizmann in establishing the Hebrew University of Jerusalem.

Einstein always appeared to have a clear view of the problems of physics and the determination to solve them. He had a strategy of his own and was able to visualize the main stages on the way to his goal. He regarded his major achievements as mere stepping-stones for the next advance.

At the start of his scientific work, Einstein realized the inadequacies of Newtonian mechanics and his special theory of relativity stemmed from an attempt to reconcile the laws of mechanics with the laws of the electromagnetic field. He dealt with classical problems of statistical mechanics and problems in which they were merged with quantum theory: this led to an explanation of the Brownian movement of molecules. He investigated the thermal properties of light with a low radiation density and his observations laid the foundation of the photon theory of light.

In his early days in Berlin, Einstein postulated that the correct interpretation of the special theory of relativity must also furnish a theory of gravitation and in 1916 he published his paper on the general theory of relativity. During this time he also contributed to the problems of the theory of radiation and statistical mechanics.

In the 1920s, Einstein embarked on the construction of unified field theories, although he continued to work on the probabilistic interpretation of quantum theory, and he persevered with this work in America. He contributed to statistical mechanics by his development of the quantum theory of a monatomic gas and he has also accomplished valuable work in connection with atomic transition probabilities and relativistic cosmology.

After his retirement he continued to work towards the unification of the basic concepts of physics, taking the opposite approach, geometrisation, to the majority of physicists.

Einstein's researches are, of course, well chronicled and his more important works include Special Theory of Relativity (1905), Relativity (English translations, 1920 and 1950), General Theory of Relativity (1916), Investigations on Theory of Brownian Movement (1926), and The Evolution of Physics (1938). Among his non-scientific works, About Zionism (1930), Why War? (1933), My Philosophy (1934), and Out of My Later Years (1950) are perhaps the most important.

Albert Einstein received honorary doctorate degrees in science, medicine and philosophy from many European and American universities. During the 1920's he lectured in Europe, America and the Far East, and he was awarded Fellowships or Memberships of all the leading scientific academies throughout the world. He gained numerous awards in recognition of his work, including the Copley Medal of the Royal Society of London in 1925, and the Franklin Medal of the Franklin Institute in 1935.

Einstein's gifts inevitably resulted in his dwelling much in intellectual solitude and, for relaxation, music played an important part in his life. He married Mileva Maric in 1903 and they had a daughter and two sons; their marriage was dissolved in 1919 and in the same year he married his cousin, Elsa Löwenthal, who died in 1936. He died on April 18, 1955 at Princeton, New Jersey.

CHAPTER THREE

Isaac Newton

Isaac Newton

Isaac Newton, in full Sir Isaac Newton, (born December 25, 1642 [January 4, 1643, New Style], Woolsthorpe, Lincolnshire, England—died March 20 [March 31], 1727, London), English physicist and mathematician, who was the culminating figure of the Scientific Revolution of the 17th century. In optics, his discovery of the composition of white light integrated the phenomena of colours into the science of light and laid the foundation for modern physical optics. In mechanics, his three laws of motion, the basic principles of modern physics, resulted in the formulation of the law of universal gravitation. In mathematics, he was the original discoverer of the infinitesimal calculus. Newton's Philosophiae Naturalis Principia Mathematica (Mathematical Principles of Natural Philosophy, 1687) was one of the most important single works in the history of modern science.

Born in the hamlet of Woolsthorpe, Newton was the only son of a local yeoman, also Isaac Newton, who had died three months before, and of Hannah Ayscough. That same year, at Arcetri near Florence, Galileo Galilei had died; Newton would eventually pick up his idea of a mathematical science of motion and bring his work to full fruition. A tiny and weak baby, Newton was not expected to survive his first day of life, much less 84 years. Deprived of a father before birth, he soon lost his mother as well, for within two years she married a second time; her husband, the well-to-do minister Barnabas Smith, left young Isaac with his grandmother and moved to a neighbouring village to raise a son and two daughters. For nine years, until the death of Barnabas Smith in 1653, Isaac was effectively separated from his mother, and his pronounced psychotic tendencies have been ascribed to this traumatic event. That he hated his stepfather we may be sure. When he examined the state of his soul in 1662 and compiled a catalog of sins in shorthand, he remembered "Threatning my father and mother Smith to burne them and the house over them." The acute sense of insecurity that rendered him obsessively anxious when his work was published and irrationally violent when he defended it accompanied Newton throughout his life and can plausibly be traced to his early years.

After his mother was widowed a second time, she determined that her first-born son should manage her now considerable property. It quickly became apparent, however, that this would be a disaster, both for the estate and for Newton. He could not bring himself to concentrate on rural affairs—set to watch the cattle, he would curl up under a tree with a book. Fortunately, the mistake was recognized, and Newton was sent back to the grammar school in Grantham, where he had already studied, to prepare for the university. As with many of the leading scientists of the age, he left behind in Grantham anecdotes about his mechanical ability and his skill in building models of machines, such as clocks and windmills. At the school he apparently gained a firm command of Latin but probably received no more than a smattering of arithmetic. By June 1661 he was ready to matriculate at Trinity College, Cambridge, somewhat older than the other undergraduates because of his interrupted education.

When Newton arrived in Cambridge in 1661, the movement now known as the Scientific Revolution was well advanced, and many of the works basic to modern science had appeared. Astronomers from Nicolaus Copernicus to Johannes Kepler had elaborated the heliocentric system of the universe.

Galileo had proposed the foundations of a new mechanics built on the principle of inertia. Led by René Descartes, philosophers had begun to formulate a new conception of nature as an intricate, impersonal, and inert machine. Yet as far as the universities of Europe, including Cambridge, were concerned, all this might well have never happened. They continued to be the strongholds of outmoded Aristotelianism, which rested on a geocentric view of the universe and dealt with nature in qualitative rather than quantitative terms.

Like thousands of other undergraduates, Newton began his higher education by immersing himself in Aristotle's work. Even though the new philosophy was not in the curriculum, it was in the air. Some time during his undergraduate career, Newton discovered the works of the French natural philosopher Descartes and the other mechanical philosophers, who, in contrast to Aristotle, viewed physical reality as composed entirely of particles of matter in motion and who held that all the phenomena of nature result from their mechanical interaction. A new set of notes, which he entitled "Quaestiones Quaedam Philosophicae" ("Certain Philosophical Questions"), begun sometime in 1664, usurped the unused pages of a notebook intended for traditional scholastic exercises; under the title he entered the slogan "Amicus Plato amicus Aristoteles magis amica veritas" ("Plato is my friend, Aristotle is my friend, but my best friend is truth"). Newton's scientific career had begun.

The "Quaestiones" reveal that Newton had discovered the new conception of nature that provided the framework of the Scientific Revolution. He had thoroughly mastered the works of Descartes and had also discovered that the French philosopher Pierre Gassendi had revived atomism, an alternative mechanical system to explain nature. The "Quaestiones" also reveal that Newton already was inclined to find the latter a more attractive philosophy than Cartesian natural philosophy, which rejected the existence of ultimate indivisible particles. The works of the 17th-century chemist Robert Boyle provided the foundation for Newton's considerable work in chemistry. Significantly, he had read Henry More, the Cambridge Platonist, and was thereby introduced to another intellectual world, the magical Hermetic tradition, which sought to explain natural phenomena in terms of alchemical and magical concepts. The two traditions of natural philosophy, the mechanical and the Hermetic, antithetical though they appear, continued to influence his thought and in their tension supplied the fundamental theme of his scientific career.

Although he did not record it in the "Quaestiones," Newton had also begun his mathematical studies. He again started with Descartes, from whose La Géometrie he branched out into the other literature of modern analysis with its application of algebraic techniques to problems of geometry. He then reached back for the support of classical geometry. Within little more than a year, he had mastered the literature; and, pursuing his own line of analysis, he began to move into new territory. He discovered the binomial theorem, and he developed the calculus, a more powerful form of analysis that employs infinitesimal considerations in finding the slopes of curves and areas under curves.

By 1669 Newton was ready to write a tract summarizing his progress, De Analysi per Aequationes Numeri Terminorum Infinitas ("On Analysis by Infinite Series"), which circulated in manuscript through a limited circle and made his name known. During the next two years he revised it as De methodis serierum et fluxionum ("On the Methods of Series and Fluxions"). The word fluxions, Newton's private rubric, indicates that the calculus had been born. Despite the fact that only a handful of savants were even aware of Newton's existence, he had arrived at the point where he had become the leading mathematician in Europe.

When Newton received the bachelor's degree in April 1665, the most remarkable undergraduate career in the history of university education had passed unrecognized. On his own, without formal guidance, he had sought out the new philosophy and the new mathematics and made them his own, but he had confined the progress of his studies to his notebooks. Then, in 1665, the plague closed the university, and for most of the following two years he was forced to stay at his home, contemplating at leisure what he had learned. During the plague years Newton laid the foundations of the calculus and extended an earlier insight into an essay, "Of Colours," which contains most of the ideas elaborated in his Opticks. It was during this time that he examined the elements of circular motion and, applying his analysis to the Moon and the planets, derived the inverse square relation that the radially directed force acting on a planet decreases with the square of its distance from the Sun—which was later crucial to the law of universal gravitation. The world heard nothing of these discoveries.

Newton was elected to a fellowship in Trinity College in 1667, after the university reopened. Two years later, Isaac Barrow, Lucasian professor of mathematics, who had transmitted Newton's De Analysi to John Collins in London, resigned the chair to devote himself to divinity and recommended

Newton to succeed him. The professorship exempted Newton from the necessity of tutoring but imposed the duty of delivering an annual course of lectures. He chose the work he had done in optics as the initial topic; during the following three years (1670–72), his lectures developed the essay "Of Colours" into a form which was later revised to become Book One of his Opticks.

Beginning with Kepler's Paralipomena in 1604, the study of optics had been a central activity of the Scientific Revolution. Descartes's statement of the sine law of refraction, relating the angles of incidence and emergence at interfaces of the media through which light passes, had added a new mathematical regularity to the science of light, supporting the conviction that the universe is constructed according to mathematical regularities. Descartes had also made light central to the mechanical philosophy of nature; the reality of light, he argued, consists of motion transmitted through a material medium. Newton fully accepted the mechanical nature of light, although he chose the atomistic alternative and held that light consists of material corpuscles in motion. The corpuscular conception of light was always a speculative theory on the periphery of his optics, however. The core of Newton's contribution had to do with colours. An ancient theory extending back at least to Aristotle held that a certain class of colour phenomena, such as the rainbow, arises from the modification of light, which appears white in its pristine form. Descartes had generalized this theory for all colours and translated it into mechanical imagery. Through a series of experiments performed in 1665 and 1666, in which the spectrum of a narrow beam was projected onto the wall of a darkened chamber, Newton denied the concept of modification and replaced it with that of analysis. Basically, he denied that light is simple and homogeneous—stating instead that it is complex and heterogeneous and that the phenomena of colours arise from the analysis of the heterogeneous mixture into its simple components. The ultimate source of Newton's conviction that light is corpuscular was his recognition that individual rays of light have immutable properties; in his view, such properties imply immutable particles of matter. He held that individual rays (that is, particles of given size) excite sensations of individual colours when they strike the retina of the eye. He also concluded that rays refract at distinct angles—hence, the prismatic spectrum, a beam of heterogeneous rays, i.e., alike incident on one face of a prism, separated or analyzed by the refraction into its component parts—and that phenomena such as the rainbow are produced by refractive analysis. Because he believed that chromatic aberration could never be eliminated from lenses, Newton turned to reflecting telescopes; he constructed the first ever built. The heterogeneity of light has been the foundation of physical optics since his time.

CHAPTER FOUR

Dr. A.P.J. Abdul Kalam

Dr. A.P.J. Abdul Kalam

A.P.J. Abdul Kalam, in full Avul Pakir Jainulabdeen Abdul Kalam, (born October 15, 1931, Rameswaram, India—died July 27, 2015, Shillong), Indian scientist and politician who played a leading role in the development of India's missile and nuclear weapons programs. He was president of India from 2002 to 2007.

Kalam earned a degree in aeronautical engineering from the Madras Institute of Technology and in 1958 joined the Defence Research and Development Organisation (DRDO). In 1969 he moved to the Indian Space Research Organisation, where he was project director of the SLV-III, the first satellite launch vehicle that was both designed and produced in India. Rejoining DRDO in 1982, Kalam planned the program that produced a number of successful missiles, which helped earn him the nickname "Missile Man." Among those successes was Agni, India's first intermediate-range ballistic missile, which incorporated aspects of the SLV-III and was launched in 1989.

From 1992 to 1997 Kalam was scientific adviser to the defense minister, and he later served as principal scientific adviser (1999–2001) to the government with the rank of cabinet minister. His prominent role in the country's 1998 nuclear weapons tests solidified India as a nuclear power and established Kalam as a national hero, although the tests caused great concern in the international community. In 1998 Kalam put forward a countrywide plan called Technology Vision 2020, which he described as a road map for transforming India from a less-developed to a developed society in 20 years. The plan called for, among other measures, increasing agricultural productivity, emphasizing technology as a vehicle for economic growth, and widening access to health care and education.

In 2002 India's ruling National Democratic Alliance (NDA) put forward Kalam to succeed outgoing President Kocheril Raman Narayanan. Kalam was nominated by the Hindu nationalist (Hindutva) NDA even though he was Muslim, and his stature and popular appeal were such that even the main opposition party, the Indian National Congress, also proposed his candidacy. Kalam easily won the election and was sworn in as India's 11th president, a largely ceremonial post, in July 2002. He left office at the end of his term in 2007 and was succeeded by Pratibha Patil, the country's first woman president.

Upon returning to civilian life, Kalam remained committed to using science and technology to transform India into a developed country and served as a lecturer at several universities. On July 27, 2015, he collapsed while delivering a lecture at the Indian Institute of Management Shillong and was pronounced dead from cardiac arrest soon afterward.

Kalam wrote several books, including an autobiography, Wings of Fire (1999). Among his numerous awards were two of the country's highest honours, the Padma Vibhushan (1990) and the Bharat Ratna (1997).

CHAPTER FIVE

Dr. B.R. Ambedkar

Dr. B.R. Ambedkar

Bhimrao Ramji Ambedkar (14 April 1891 – 6 December 1956) was an Indian jurist, economist, social reformer and political leader who headed the committee drafting the Constitution of India from the Constituent Assembly debates, served as Law and Justice minister in the first cabinet of Jawaharlal Nehru, and inspired the Dalit Buddhist movement after renouncing Hinduism.

Ambedkar graduated from Elphinstone College, University of Bombay, and studied economics at Columbia University and the London School of Economics, receiving doctorates in 1927 and 1923 respectively and was among a handful of Indian students to have done so at either institution in the 1920s.[13] He also trained in the law at Gray's Inn, London. In his early career, he was an economist, professor, and lawyer. His later life was marked by his political activities; he became involved in campaigning and negotiations for India's independence, publishing journals, advocating political rights and social freedom for Dalits, and contributing significantly to the establishment of the state of India. In 1956, he converted to Buddhism, initiating mass conversions of Dalits.[14]

In 1990, the Bharat Ratna, India's highest civilian award, was posthumously conferred on Ambedkar. The salutation Jai Bhim (lit. "Hail Bhim") used by followers honours him. He is also referred to by the honorific Babasaheb (BAH-bə SAH-hayb).

Ambedkar was born on 14 April 1891 in the town and military cantonment of Mhow (now officially known as Dr Ambedkar Nagar) (now in Madhya Pradesh).[15] He was the 14th and last child of Ramji Maloji Sakpal, an army officer who held the rank of Subedar, and Bhimabai Sakpal, daughter of Laxman Murbadkar.[16] His family was of Marathi background from the town of Ambadawe (Mandangad taluka) in Ratnagiri district of modern-day Maharashtra. Ambedkar was born into a Mahar (dalit) caste, who were treated as untouchables and subjected to socio-economic discrimination.[17] Ambedkar's ancestors had long worked for the army of the British East India Company, and his father served in the British Indian Army at the Mhow cantonment.[18] Although they attended school, Ambedkar and other untouchable children were segregated and given little attention or help by teachers. They were not allowed to sit inside the class. When they needed to drink water, someone from a higher caste had to pour that water from a height as they were not allowed to touch either the water or the vessel that contained it. This task was usually performed for the young Ambedkar by the school peon, and if the peon was not available then he had to go without water; he described the situation later in his writings as "No peon, No Water".[19] He was required to sit on a gunny sack which he had to take home with him.[20]

Ramji Sakpal retired in 1894 and the family moved to Satara two years later. Shortly after their move, Ambedkar's mother died. The children were cared for by their paternal aunt and lived in difficult circumstances. Three sons – Balaram, Anandrao and Bhimrao – and two daughters – Manjula and Tulasa – of the Ambedkars survived them. Of his brothers and sisters, only Ambedkar passed his examinations and went to high school. His original surname was Sakpal but his father registered his name as Ambadawekar in school, meaning he comes from his native village 'Ambadawe' in Ratnagiri district.[21][22][23][24] His Marathi Brahmin teacher, Krishnaji Keshav Ambedkar, changed his surname from 'Ambadawekar' to his own surname 'Ambedkar' in school records .

In 1897, Ambedkar's family moved to Mumbai where Ambedkar became the only untouchable enrolled at Elphinstone High School. In 1906, when he was about 15 years old, he married a nine-year-old girl, Ramabai. The match per the customs prevailing at that time was arranged by the couple's parents .

n 1907, he passed his matriculation examination and in the following year he entered Elphinstone College, which was affiliated to the University of Bombay, becoming, according to him, the first from his Mahar caste to do so. When he passed his English fourth standard examinations, the people of his community wanted to celebrate because they considered that he had reached "great heights" which he says was "hardly an occasion compared to the state of education in other communities". A public ceremony was evoked, to celebrate his success, by the community, and it was at this occasion that he was presented with a biography of the Buddha by Dada Keluskar, the author and a family friend.[31]

By 1912, he obtained his degree in economics and political science from Bombay University, and prepared to take up employment with the Baroda state government. His wife had just moved his young family and started work when he had to quickly return to Mumbai to see his ailing father, who died on 2 February 1913.

In 1913, at the age of 22, Ambedkar was awarded a Baroda State Scholarship of £11.50 (Sterling) per month for three years under a scheme established by Sayajirao Gaekwad III (Gaekwad of Baroda) that was designed to provide opportunities for postgraduate education at Columbia University in New York City. Soon after arriving there he settled in rooms at Livingston Hall with Naval Bhathena, a Parsi who was to be a lifelong friend. He passed his M.A. exam in June 1915, majoring in economics, and other subjects of Sociology, History, Philosophy and Anthropology. He presented a thesis, Ancient Indian Commerce. Ambedkar was influenced by John Dewey and his work on democracy.[33]

In 1916, he completed his second master's thesis, National Dividend of India – A Historic and Analytical Study, for a second M.A.[34] On 9 May, he presented the paper Castes in India: Their Mechanism, Genesis and

Development before a seminar conducted by the anthropologist Alexander Goldenweiser. Ambedkar received his Ph.D. degree in economics at Columbia in 1927.

In October 1916, he enrolled for the Bar course at Gray's Inn, and at the same time enrolled at the London School of Economics where he started working on a doctoral thesis. In June 1917, he returned to India because his scholarship from Baroda ended. His book collection was dispatched on a different ship from the one he was on, and that ship was torpedoed and sunk by a German submarine.[32] He got permission to return to London to submit his thesis within four years. He returned at the first opportunity, and completed a master's degree in 1921. His thesis was on "The problem of the rupee: Its origin and its solution".[35] In 1923, he completed a D.Sc. in Economics which was awarded from University of London, and the same year he was called to the Bar by Gray's Inn.

As Ambedkar was educated by the Princely State of Baroda, he was bound to serve it. He was appointed Military Secretary to the Gaikwad but had to quit in a short time. He described the incident in his autobiography, Waiting for a Visa.[36] Thereafter, he tried to find ways to make a living for his growing family. He worked as a private tutor, as an accountant, and established an investment consulting business, but it failed when his clients learned that he was an untouchable.[37] In 1918, he became Professor of Political Economy in the Sydenham College of Commerce and Economics in Mumbai. Although he was successful with the students, other professors objected to his sharing a drinking-water jug with them.[38]

Ambedkar had been invited to testify before the Southborough Committee, which was preparing the Government of India Act 1919. At this hearing, Ambedkar argued for creating separate electorates and reservations for untouchables and other religious communities.[39] In 1920, he began the publication of the weekly Mooknayak (Leader of the Silent) in Mumbai with the help of Shahu of Kolhapur, that is, Shahu IV (1874–1922).[40]

Ambedkar went on to work as a legal professional. In 1926, he successfully defended three non-Brahmin leaders who had accused the Brahmin community of ruining India and were then subsequently sued for libel. Dhananjay Keer notes, "The victory was resounding, both socially and individually, for the clients and the doctor".

While practising law in the Bombay High Court, he tried to promote education to untouchables and uplift them. His first organised attempt was his establishment of the central institution Bahishkrit Hitakarini Sabha, intended to promote education and socio-economic improvement, as well as the welfare of "outcastes", at the time referred to as depressed classes.[41] For the defence of Dalit rights, he started many periodicals like Mook Nayak, Bahishkrit Bharat, and Equality Janta.[42]

He was appointed to the Bombay Presidency Committee to work with the all-European Simon Commission in 1925.[43] This commission had sparked great protests across India, and while its report was ignored by most Indians, Ambedkar himself wrote a separate set of recommendations for the future Constitution of India.[44]

By 1927, Ambedkar had decided to launch active movements against untouchability. He began with public movements and marches to open up public drinking water resources. He also began a struggle for the right to enter Hindu temples. He led a satyagraha in Mahad to fight for the right of the untouchable community to draw water from the main water tank of the town.[45] In a conference in late 1927, Ambedkar publicly condemned the classic Hindu text, the Manusmriti (Laws of Manu), for ideologically justifying caste discrimination and "untouchability", and he ceremonially burned copies of the ancient text. On 25 December 1927, he led thousands of followers to burn copies of Manusmriti.[46][47] Thus annually 25 December is celebrated as Manusmriti Dahan Din (Manusmriti Burning Day) by Ambedkarites and Dalits.[48][49]

In 1930, Ambedkar launched the Kalaram Temple movement after three months of preparation. About 15,000 volunteers assembled at Kalaram Temple satygraha making one of the greatest processions of Nashik. The procession was headed by a military band and a batch of scouts; women and men walked with discipline, order and determination to see the god for the first time. When they reached the gates, the gates were closed by Brahmin authorities.

In 1932, the British colonial government announced the formation of a separate electorate for "Depressed Classes" in the Communal Award. Mahatma Gandhi fiercely opposed a separate electorate for untouchables, saying he feared that such an arrangement would divide the Hindu community.[51][52][53] Gandhi protested by fasting while imprisoned in the Yerwada Central Jail of Poona. Following the fast, congressional politicians and activists such as Madan Mohan Malaviya and Palwankar Baloo organised joint meetings with Ambedkar and his supporters at Yerwada.[54] On 25 September 1932, the agreement, known as the Poona

Pact was signed between Ambedkar (on behalf of the depressed classes among Hindus) and Madan Mohan Malaviya (on behalf of the other Hindus). The agreement gave reserved seats for the depressed classes in the Provisional legislatures within the general electorate. Due to the pact the depressed class received 148 seats in the legislature instead of the 71, as allocated in the Communal Award proposed earlier by the colonial government under Prime Minister Ramsay MacDonald. The text used the term "Depressed Classes" to denote Untouchables among Hindus who were later called Scheduled Castes and Scheduled Tribes under the India Act 1935, and the later Indian Constitution of 1950.[55] In the Poona Pact, a unified electorate was in principle formed, but primary and secondary elections allowed Untouchables in practice to choose their own candidates.

In 1935, Ambedkar was appointed principal of the Government Law College, Bombay, a position he held for two years. He also served as the chairman of Governing body of Ramjas College, University of Delhi, after the death of its Founder Shri Rai Kedarnath.[57] Settling in Bombay (today called Mumbai), Ambedkar oversaw the construction of a house, and stocked his personal library with more than 50,000 books.[58] His wife Ramabai died after a long illness the same year. It had been her long-standing wish to go on a pilgrimage to Pandharpur, but Ambedkar had refused to let her go, telling her that he would create a new Pandharpur for her instead of Hinduism's Pandharpur which treated them as untouchables. At the Yeola Conversion Conference on 13 October in Nasik, Ambedkar announced his intention to convert to a different religion and exhorted his followers to leave Hinduism.[58] He would repeat his message at many public meetings across India.

In 1936, Ambedkar founded the Independent Labour Party, which contested the 1937 Bombay election to the Central Legislative Assembly for the 13 reserved and 4 general seats, and secured 11 and 3 seats respectively.[59]

Ambedkar published his book Annihilation of Caste on 15 May 1936.[60] It strongly criticised Hindu orthodox religious leaders and the caste system in general,[61] and included "a rebuke of Gandhi" on the subject.[62] Later, in a 1955 BBC interview, he accused Gandhi of writing in opposition of the caste system in English language papers while writing in support of it in Gujarati language papers.[63]

During this time, Ambedkar also fought against the khoti system prevalent in Konkan, where khots, or government revenue collectors, regularly exploited farmers and tenants. In 1937, Ambedkar tabled a bill in the Bombay Legislative Assembly aimed at abolishing the khoti system by creating a direct relationship between government and farmers.[64]

Ambedkar served on the Defence Advisory Committee[5] and the Viceroy's Executive Council as minister for labour.[5] Before the Day of Deliverance events, Ambedkar stated that he was interested in participating: "I read Mr. Jinnah's statement and I felt ashamed to have allowed him to steal a march over me and rob me of the language and the sentiment which I, more than Mr. Jinnah, was entitled to use." He went on to suggest that the communities he worked with were twenty times more oppressed by Congress policies than were Indian Muslims; he clarified that he was criticizing Congress, and not all Hindus.[65] Jinnah and Ambedkar jointly addressed the heavily attended Day of Deliverance event in Bhindi Bazaar, Bombay, where both expressed "fiery" criticisms of the Congress party, and according to one observer, suggested that Islam and Hinduism were irreconcilable.[65][66]

After the Lahore resolution (1940) of the Muslim League demanding Pakistan, Ambedkar wrote a 400-page tract titled Thoughts on Pakistan, which analysed the concept of "Pakistan" in all its aspects. Ambedkar argued that the Hindus should concede Pakistan to the Muslims. He proposed that the provincial boundaries of Punjab and Bengal should be redrawn to separate the Muslim and non-Muslim majority parts. He thought the Muslims could have no objection to redrawing provincial boundaries. If they did, they did not quite "understand the nature of their own demand". Scholar Venkat Dhulipala states that Thoughts on Pakistan "rocked Indian politics for a decade". It determined the course of dialogue between the Muslim League and the Indian National Congress, paving the way for the Partition of India.[67][68]

In his work Who Were the Shudras?, Ambedkar tried to explain the formation of untouchables. He saw Shudras and Ati Shudras who form the lowest caste in the ritual hierarchy of the caste system, as separate from Untouchables. Ambedkar oversaw the transformation of his political party into the Scheduled Castes Federation, although it performed poorly in the 1946 elections for Constituent Assembly of India. Later he was elected into the constituent assembly of Bengal where Muslim League was in power.[2]

Ambedkar contested in the Bombay North first Indian General Election of 1952, but lost to his former assistant and Congress Party candidate Narayan Kajrolkar. Ambedkar became a member of Rajya Sabha, probably an appointed member. He tried to enter Lok Sabha again in the by-election of 1954 from Bhandara, but he placed third (the Congress Party won). By the time of the second general election in 1957, Ambedkar had died.

Ambedkar also criticised Islamic practice in South Asia. While justifying the Partition of India, he condemned child marriage and the mistreatment of women in Muslim society.

No words can adequately express the great and many evils of polygamy and concubinage, and especially as a source of misery to a Muslim woman. Take the caste system. Everybody infers that Islam must be free from slavery and caste. [...] [While slavery existed], much of its support was derived from Islam and Islamic countries. While the prescriptions by the Prophet regarding the just and humane treatment of slaves contained in the Koran are praiseworthy, there is nothing whatever in Islam that lends support to the abolition of this curse. But if slavery has gone, caste among Musalmans [Muslims] has remained.

Upon India's independence on 15 August 1947, the new prime minister Jawaharlal Nehru invited Ambedkar to serve as the Dominion of India's Law Minister; two weeks later, he was appointed Chairman of the Drafting Committee of the Constitution for the future Republic of India.

Indian constitution guarantees and protections for a wide range of civil liberties for individual citizens, including freedom of religion, the abolition of untouchability, and the outlawing of all forms of discrimination. Ambedkar argued for extensive economic and social rights for women, and won the Assembly's support for introducing a system of reservations of jobs in the civil services, schools and colleges for members of scheduled castes and scheduled tribes and Other Backward Class, a system akin to affirmative action. India's lawmakers hoped to eradicate the socio-economic inequalities and lack of opportunities for India's depressed classes through these measures.[70] The Constitution was adopted on 26 November 1949 by the Constituent Assembly.[

Ambedkar was the first Indian to pursue a doctorate in economics abroad.[72] He argued that industrialisation and agricultural growth could enhance the Indian economy.[73] He stressed investment in agriculture as the primary industry of India.[citation needed] According to Sharad Pawar, Ambedkar's vision helped the government to achieve its food security goal.[74] Ambedkar advocated national economic and social development, stressing education, public hygiene, community health, residential facilities as the basic amenities.[73] His DSc thesis, The problem of the Rupee: Its

Origin and Solution (1923) examines the causes for the Rupee's fall in value. In this dissertation, he argued in favour of a gold standard in modified form, and was opposed to the gold-exchange standard favoured by Keynes in his treatise Indian Currency and Finance (1909), claiming it was less stable. He favoured the stoppage of all further coinage of the rupee and the minting of a gold coin, which he believed would fix currency rates and prices.[75]

He also analysed revenue in his PhD dissertation The Evolution of Provincial Finance in British India. In this work, he analysed the various systems used by the British colonial government to manage finances in India.[75][76] His views on finance were that governments should ensure their expenditures have "faithfulness, wisdom and economy." "Faithfulness" meaning governments should use money as nearly as possible to the original intentions of spending the money in the first place. "Wisdom" meaning it should be used as well as possible for the public good, and "economy" meaning the funds should be used so that the maximum value can be extracted from them.[77]

In 1951, Ambedkar established the Finance Commission of India. He opposed income tax for low-income groups. He contributed in Land Revenue Tax and excise duty policies to stabilise the economy.[citation needed] He played an important role in land reform and the state economic development.[citation needed] According to him, the caste system, due to its division of labourers and hierarchical nature, impedes movement of labour (higher castes would not do lower-caste occupations) and movement of capital (assuming investors would invest first in their own caste occupation). His theory of State Socialism had three points: state ownership of agricultural land, the maintenance of resources for production by the state, and a just distribution of these resources to the population. He emphasised a free economy with a stable Rupee which India has adopted recently.[citation needed] He advocated birth control to develop the Indian economy, and this has been adopted by Indian government as national policy for family planning. He emphasised equal rights for women for economic development.[citation needed]

Ambedkar's views on agricultural land was that too much of it was idle, or that it was not being utilized properly. He believed there was an "ideal proportion" of production factors that would allow agricultural land to be used most productively. To this end, he saw the large portion of people who lived on agriculture at the time as a major problem. Therefore, he advocated industrialization of the economy to allow these agricultural labourers to be of more use elsewhere.[

Ambedkar's first wife Ramabai died in 1935 after a long illness. After completing the draft of India's constitution in the late 1940s, he suffered from lack of sleep, had neuropathic pain in his legs, and was taking insulin and homoeopathic medicines. He went to Bombay for treatment, and there met Sharada Kabir, whom he married on 15 April 1948, at his home in New Delhi. Doctors recommended a companion who was a good cook and had medical knowledge to care for him.[82] She adopted the name Savita Ambedkar and cared for him the rest of his life.[83] Savita Ambedkar, who was called also 'Mai', died on May 29, 2003, aged 93 in Mumbai

Ambedkar considered converting to Sikhism, which encouraged opposition to oppression and so appealed to leaders of scheduled castes. But after meeting with Sikh leaders, he concluded that he might get "second-rate" Sikh status.[85]

Instead, around 1950, he began devoting his attention to Buddhism and travelled to Ceylon (now Sri Lanka) to attend a meeting of the World Fellowship of Buddhists.[86] While dedicating a new Buddhist vihara near Pune, Ambedkar announced he was writing a book on Buddhism, and that when it was finished, he would formally convert to Buddhism.[87] He twice visited Burma in 1954; the second time to attend the third conference of the World Fellowship of Buddhists in Rangoon.[88] In 1955, he founded the Bharatiya Bauddha Mahasabha, or the Buddhist Society of India.[89] In 1956, he completed his final work, The Buddha and His Dhamma, which was published posthumously.[89]

After meetings with the Sri Lankan Buddhist monk Hammalawa Saddhatissa,[90] Ambedkar organised a formal public ceremony for himself and his supporters in Nagpur on 14 October 1956. Accepting the Three Refuges and Five Precepts from a Buddhist monk in the traditional manner, Ambedkar completed his own conversion, along with his wife. He then proceeded to convert some 500,000 of his supporters who were gathered around him.[87][91] He prescribed the 22 Vows for these converts, after the Three Jewels and Five Precepts. He then travelled to Kathmandu, Nepal to attend the Fourth World Buddhist Conference.[88] His work on The Buddha or Karl Marx and "Revolution and counter-revolution in ancient India" remained incomplete.

Since 1948, Ambedkar had diabetes. He remained in bed from June to October in 1954 due to medication side-effects and poor eyesight.[87]

His health worsened during 1955. Three days after completing his final manuscript The Buddha and His Dhamma, Ambedkar died in his sleep on 6 December 1956 at his home in Delhi.[citation needed]

A Buddhist cremation was organised at Dadar Chowpatty beach on 7 December,[92] attended by half a million grieving people.[93] A conversion program was organised on 16 December 1956,[94] so that cremation attendees were also converted to Buddhism at the same place.[94]

Ambedkar was survived by his second wife Savita Ambedkar (known as Maisaheb Ambedkar), who died in 2003,[95] and his son Yashwant Ambedkar (known as Bhaiyasaheb Ambedkar), who died in 1977.[96] Savita and Yashwant carried on the socio-religious movement started by B. R. Ambedkar. Yashwant served as the 2nd President of the Buddhist Society of India (1957–1977) and a member of the Maharashtra Legislative Council (1960–1966).[97][98] Ambedkar's elder grandson, Prakash Yashwant Ambedkar, is the chief-adviser of the Buddhist Society of India,[99] leads the Vanchit Bahujan Aghadi and has served in both houses of the Indian Parliament.[101] Ambedkar's younger grandson, Anandraj Ambedkar leads the Republican Sena (tran: The "Republican Army").[102]

A number of unfinished typescripts and handwritten drafts were found among Ambedkar's notes and papers and gradually made available. Among these were Waiting for a Visa, which probably dates from 1935 to 1936 and is an autobiographical work, and the Untouchables, or the Children of India's Ghetto, which refers to the census of 1951.[87]

A memorial for Ambedkar was established in his Delhi house at 26 Alipur Road. His birthdate is celebrated as a public holiday known as Ambedkar Jayanti or Bhim Jayanti. He was posthumously awarded India's highest civilian honour, the Bharat Ratna, in 1990.[103]

On the anniversary of his birth and death, and on Dhamma Chakra Pravartan Din (14 October) at Nagpur, at least half a million people gather to pay homage to him at his memorial in Mumbai.[104] Thousands of bookshops are set up, and books are sold. His message to his followers was "educate, agitate, organise!"[105]

CHAPTER SIX

J.R.D. Tata

J.R.D. Tata

J. R. D. Tata was born as Jehangir on 29 July 1904 to a non-resident Indian Parsi family in Paris, France. He was the second child of businessman Ratanji Dadabhoy Tata and his French wife, Suzanne "Sooni" Brière.[2] His father was the first cousin of Jamsetji Tata, a pioneer industrialist in India. He had one elder sister Sylla, a younger sister Rodabeh and two younger brothers Darab and Jamshed (called Jimmy) Tata. His sister, Sylla, was married to Dinshaw Maneckji Petit, the third baronet of Petits. His sister's sister-in-law, Rattanbai Petit, was the wife of Muhammad Ali Jinnah, who later became the founder of Pakistan in August 1947. Jinnah and Rattanbai's daughter Dina Jinnah, was married to Bombay Dyeing chairman Neville Wadia who was the son of Sir Ness Wadia and Lady Eveylne Clara Powell Wadia. Neville and Dina had two children, Nusli Wadia and Diana N Wadia. Nusli is the current chairman of the Wadia Group. Nusli married Maureen Waida and they have two children, Jehangir Wadia and Ness Wadia.

As his mother was French, he spent much of his childhood in France and as a result, French was his first language. He attended the Janson De Sailly School in Paris.[3] One of the teachers at that school used to call him L'Egyptien.[4]

He attended the Cathedral and John Connon School, Bombay. Tata was educated in London, Japan, France and India.[5] When his father joined the Tata company he moved the whole family to London. During this time, J. R. D.'s mother died at the age of 43 while his father was in India and his family was in France.

After his mother's death, Ratanji Dadabhoy Tata decided to move his family to India and sent J. R. D. to England for higher studies in October 1923. He was enrolled in a grammar school, and was interested in studying engineering at Cambridge University. However, as a citizen of France J. R. D. had to enlist in the army for at least a year. In between grammar school and his time in the army, he spent a brief spell at home in Bombay. After joining the French Army he was posted into a regiment of spahis.[6] Upon discovering Tata could not only read and write French and English,[7] but could type as well, a colonel had him assigned as a secretary in his office. After his time in the French Army, his father decided to bring him back to India and he joined the Tata Company.

In 1929, Tata renounced his French citizenship and became an Indian citizen. In 1930 Tata married Thelma Vicaji, the niece of Jack Vicaji, a colourful lawyer whom he hired to defend him on a charge of driving his Bugatti too fast along Bombay's main promenade, Marine Drive. Previously he had been engaged to Dinbai Mehta, the future mother of The Economist editor Shapur Kharegat.

While he was born to a Parsi father, and his French mother converted to Zoroastrianism, J. R. D. was agnostic. He found some Parsi religious customs like their funeral rites and their exclusiveness irksome. He adhered to the three basic tenets of Zoroastrianism, which were good thoughts, good words, and good deeds, but he did not profess belief or disbelief in God.[8]

When Tata was in tour, he was inspired by his friend's father, aviation pioneer Louis Blériot, the first man to fly across the English Channel, and took to flying. On 10 February 1929, Tata obtained the first license issued in India.[9] He later came to be known as the "Father of Indian civil aviation". He founded India's first commercial airline, Tata Airlines in 1932, which became Air India in 1946, now India's national airline. He and Nevill Vintcent worked together in building Tata Airlines. They were also good friends. In 1929, J. R. D. became one of the first Indians to be granted a commercial's license. In 1932 Tata Aviation Service, the forerunner to Tata Airline and Air India, took to the skies.[citation needed] That same year he flew the first commercial mail flight to Juhu, in a de Havilland Puss Moth.[10]

The first flight in the History of Indian aviation lifted off from Drigh in Karachi to Madras with J. R. D. at the controls of a Puss on 15 October 1932.[11] J. R. D. nourished and nurtured his airline baby through to 1953, when the government of Jawaharlal Nehru nationalised Air India. It was a decision J. R. D. had fought against tooth and nail.[citation needed]

He joined Tata Sons as an unpaid apprentice in 1925. In 1938, at the age of 34, Tata was elected Chairman of Tata Sons making him the head of the largest industrial group in India. He took over as Chairman of Tata Sons from his second cousin Nowroji Saklatwala. For decades, he directed the huge Tata Group of companies, with major interests in steel, engineering, power, chemicals and hospitality. He was famous for succeeding in business while maintaining high ethical standards – refusing to bribe politicians or use the black market.

Under his chairmanship, the assets of the Tata Group grew from US$100 million to over US$5 billion. He started with 14 enterprises under his leadership and half a century later on 26 July 1988, when he left, Tata Sons was a conglomerate of 95 enterprises which they either started or in which they had controlling interest.

He was the trustee of the Sir Dorabji Tata Trust from its inception in 1932 for over half a century. Under his guidance, this Trust established Asia's first cancer facility, the Tata Memorial Centre for Cancer, Research and Treatment, in Bombay in 1941. He also founded the Tata Institute of Social Sciences (TISS, 1936), the Tata Institute of Fundamental Research (TIFR, 1945), and the National Center for Performing Arts.

In 1945, he founded Tata Motors. In 1948, Tata launched Air India International as India's first international airline. In 1953, the Indian Government appointed Tata as Chairman of Air India and a director on the Board of Indian Airlines – a position he retained for 25 years. For his crowning achievements in aviation, he was bestowed with the title of Honorary Air Commodore of India.

Tata cared greatly for his workers. In 1956, he initiated a programme of closer 'employee association with management' to give workers a stronger voice in the affairs of the company. He firmly believed in employee welfare and espoused the principles of an eight-hour working day, free medical aid, workers' provident scheme, and workmen's accident compensation schemes, which were later, adopted as statutory requirements in India.

He was also a founding member of the first Governing Body of NCAER, the National Council of Applied Economic Research in New Delhi, India's first independent economic policy institute established in 1956. In 1968, he founded Tata Consultancy Services as Tata Computer Centre. In 1979, Tata Steel instituted a new practice: a worker being deemed to be "at work" from the moment he leaves home for work until he returns home from work. This made the company financially liable to the worker for any mishap on the way to and from work. In 1987, he founded Titan Industries. Jamshedpur was also selected as a UN Global Compact City because of the quality of life, conditions of sanitation, roads and welfare that were offered by Tata Steel.

Tata was also controversially supportive of the declaration of emergency powers by Prime Minister, Indira Gandhi, in 1975. He is quoted to have told a reporter of the Times, "things had gone too far. You can't imagine what we've been through here—strikes, boycotts, demonstrations. Why, there were days I couldn't walk out of my house into the streets. The parliamentary system is not suited to our needs."

Tata received a number of awards. He was conferred the honorary rank of group captain by the Indian Air Force in 1948, was promoted to the Air Commodore rank (equivalent to Brigadier in the army) on 4 October 1966, and was further promoted on 1 April 1974 to the Air Vice Marshal rank. Several international awards for aviation were given to him – the Tony Jannus Award in March 1979, the Gold Air Medal of the Federation Aeronautique International in 1985, the Edward Warner Award of the International Civil Aviation Organisation, Canada in 1986 and the Daniel Guggenheim Medal in 1988. He received the Padma Vibhushan in 1955. The French Legion of Honour was bestowed on him in 1983. In 1992, because of his selfless humanitarian endeavours, Tata was awarded India's highest civilian honour, the Bharat Ratna. In the same year, Tata was also bestowed with the United Nations Population Award for his crusading endeavours towards initiating and successfully implementing the family planning movement in India, much before it became an official government policy. In his memory, the Government of Maharashtra named its first double-decker bridge the Bharatratna JRD Tata Overbridge at Nasik Phata, Pimpri Chinchwad.

Tata died in Geneva, Switzerland on 29 November 1993 at the age of 89 of a kidney infection. He said a few days before his passing: "Comme c'est doux de mourir" ("How gentle it is to die").

Upon his death, the Indian Parliament was adjourned in his memory – an honour not usually given to persons who are not members of parliament. He was buried at the Père Lachaise Cemetery in Paris.

In 2012, Tata was ranked the sixth "The Greatest Indian" in an Outlook magazine poll, "conducted in conjunction with CNN-IBN and History18 Channels with BBC.

www.ingramcontent.com/pod-product-compliance
Lightning Source LLC
Chambersburg PA
CBHW050817160726
48004CB00002B/881